Pre-reader

At the Beach

Shira Evans

NATIONAL
GEOGRAPHIC

Washington, D.C.

Vocabulary Tree

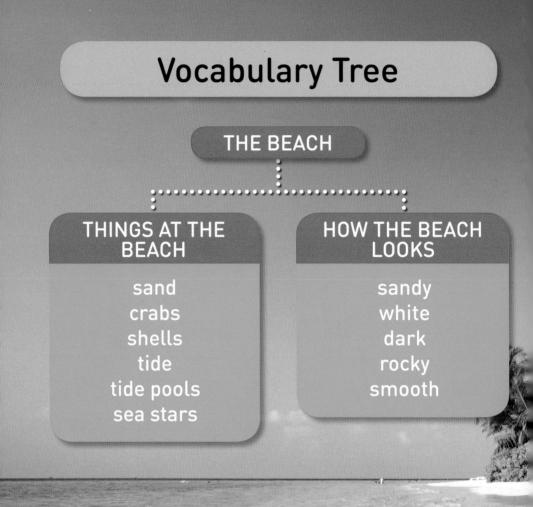

THE BEACH

THINGS AT THE BEACH

sand
crabs
shells
tide
tide pools
sea stars

HOW THE BEACH LOOKS

sandy
white
dark
rocky
smooth

The beach is by the ocean.
It's sandy.

Some beaches have white sand.

Some beaches have
dark sand.

Some beaches are rocky.

Some beaches are smooth.

Crabs live at the beach.

Some beaches have big crabs.

Some beaches have
small crabs.

There are different shells

on the beach, too.

The beach keeps changing.
The tide can be high.

Or it can be low.

When it's high tide,
there is a lot of water.

When it's low tide,
there is less water.

Some beaches have tide pools

when it's low tide.

In a tide pool, you can see sea stars

and seaweed.

Soon it will be high tide, and the beach will change again.

YOUR TURN!

Describe each beach.
Use the words below.

white sand   rocky   tide pool

smooth   dark sand

23

The publisher gratefully acknowledges the expert literacy review of this book by Kimberly Gillow, Principal, Milan Area Schools, Michigan.

Published by National Geographic Partners, LLC, Washington, D.C. 20036.

Designed by Sanjida Rashid

Trade paperback ISBN: 978-1-4263-2807-7
Reinforced library binding ISBN: 978-1-4263-2808-4

Photo Credits
Cover, Spanishalex/Getty Images; 1 (CTR), Aliaksandr Mazurkevich/Alamy Stock Photo; 2–3 (CTR), Matteo Colombo/Getty Images; 4 (CTR), tommasolizzul/Getty Images; 5 (CTR), Philip Rosenberg/Getty Images; 6 (CTR), Ian Trower/AWL Images Ltd/Getty Images; 7 (CTR), ronniechua/Getty Images; 8–9 (CTR), Photon-Photos/Getty Images; 10 (CTR), Morales/Getty Images; 11 (CTR), Colin Marshall/Minden Pictures; 12–13 (CTR), Arco Images/Alamy Stock Photo; 14–15 (CTR), Michael Marten; 16–17 (CTR), Michael Marten; 18–19 (CTR), John White Photos/Getty Images; 20 (CTR), Craig Tuttle/Getty Images; 21 (CTR), Richard Fairless/Getty Images; 22 (CTR), Ralph Lee Hopkins/National Geographic Creative; 23 (UP LE), danilovi/Getty Images; 23 (UP RT), Michael Marfell/Getty Images; 23 (LO LE), Sirachai Arunrugstichai/Getty Images; 23 (LO RT), Glow Images, Inc/Getty Images; 23 (LO), Colin Monteath/Minden Pictures; 24 (UP), M Swiet Productions/Getty Images

National Geographic supports K–12 educators with ELA Common Core Resources. Visit natgeoed.org/commoncore for more information.

Printed in the United States of America
17/WOR/1